IDW®
www.IDWPUBLISHING.com

Ted Adams, CEO & Publisher • **Greg Goldstein,** President & COO

Robbie Robbins, EVP/Sr. Graphic Artist • **Chris Ryall,** Chief Creative Officer

David Hedgecock, Editor-in-Chief • **Laurie Windrow,** Senior Vice President of Sales & Marketing

Matthew Ruzicka, CPA, Chief Financial Officer • **Lorelei Bunjes,** VP of Digital Services

Jerry Bennington, VP of New Product Development

Facebook: **facebook.com/idwpublishing**
Twitter: **@idwpublishing**
YouTube: **youtube.com/idwpublishing**
Tumblr: **tumblr.idwpublishing.com**
Instagram: **instagram.com/idwpublishing**

This book belongs to...

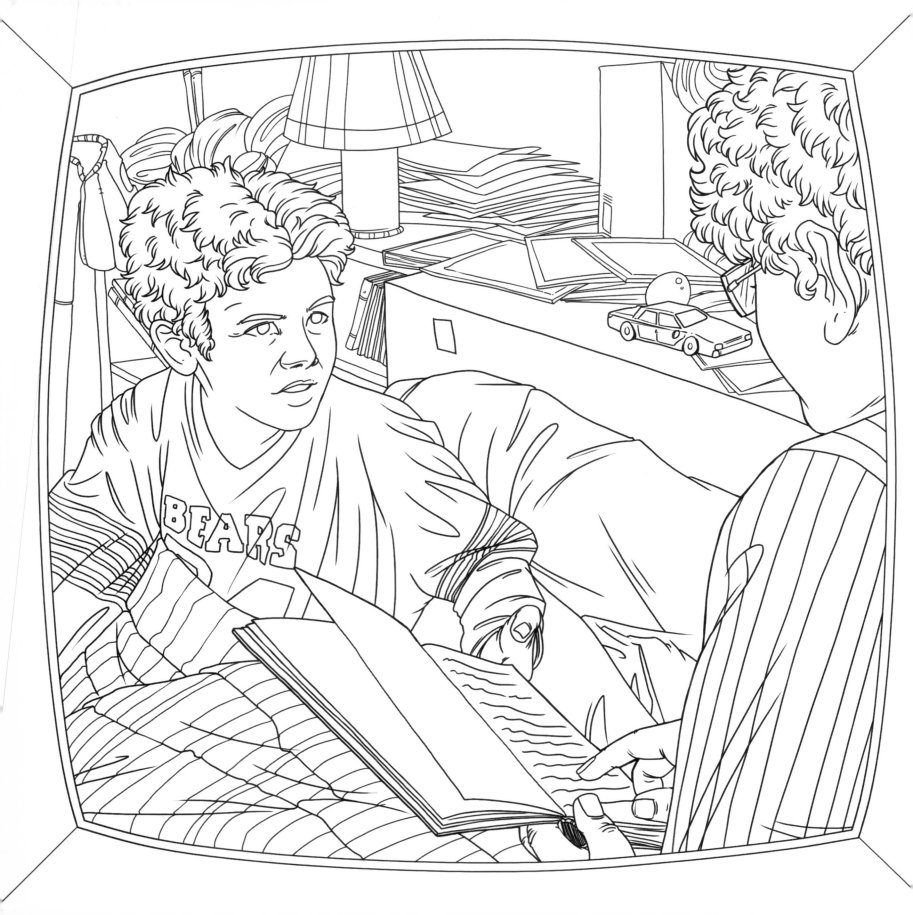

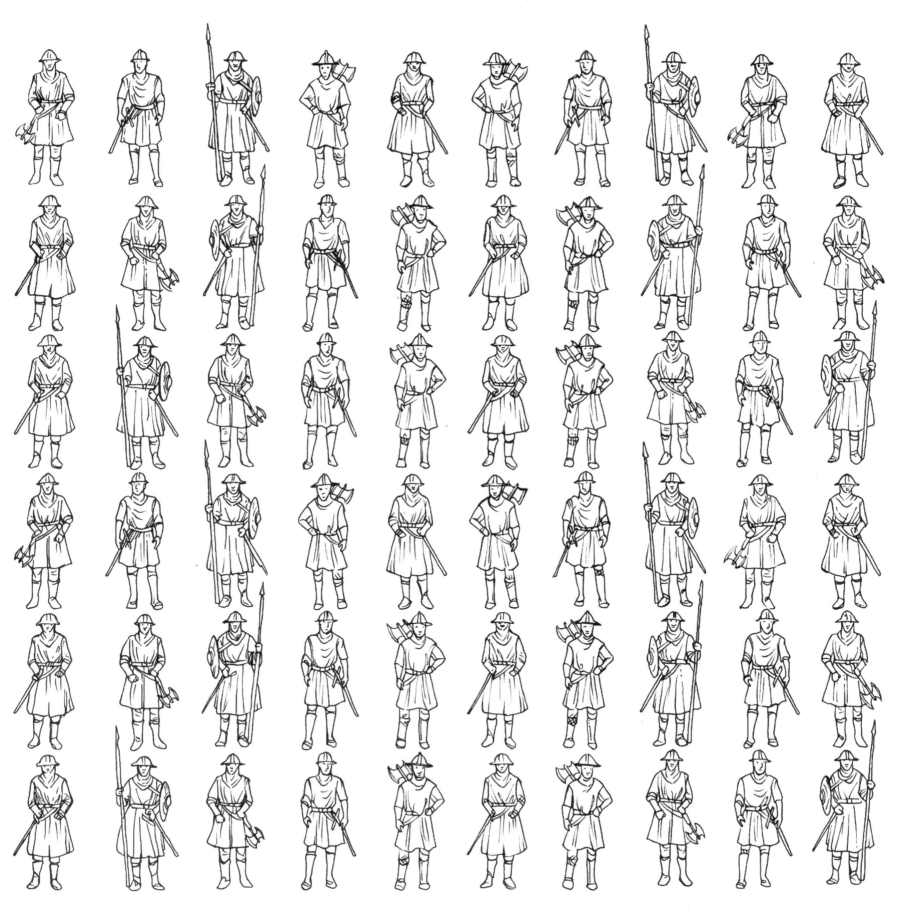

THERE'S A SHORTAGE OF PERFECT
BREASTS IN THIS WORLD

IT WOULD BE A PITY TO
DAMAGE YOURS

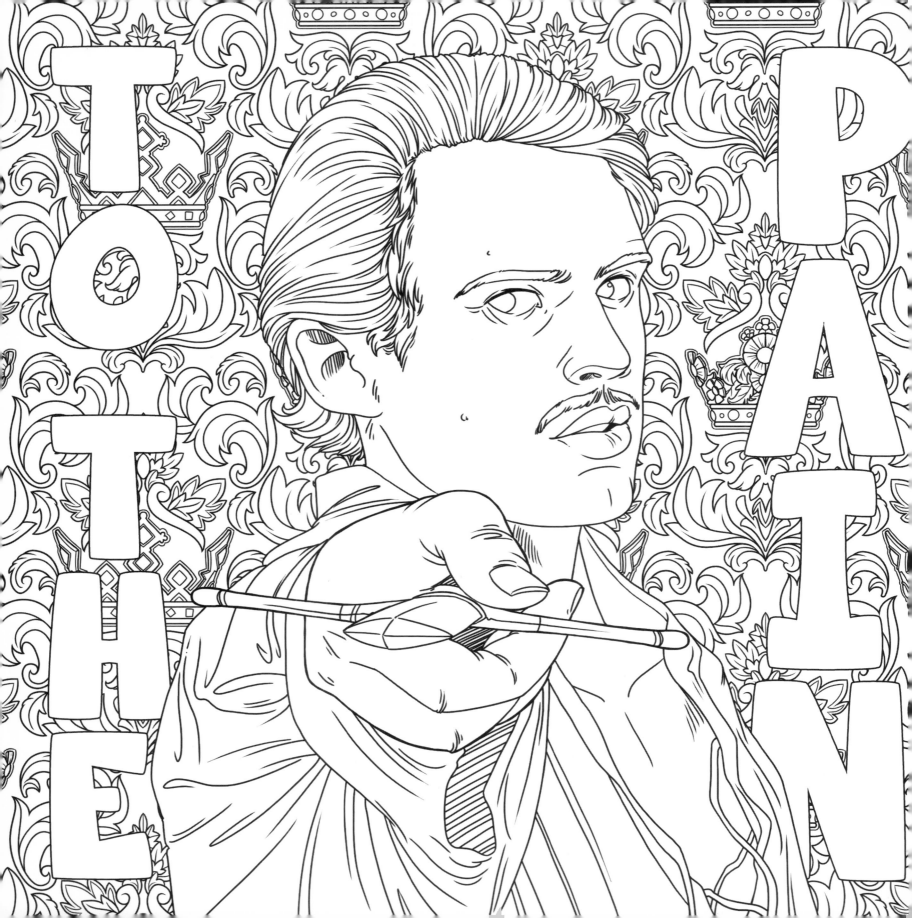

Create Your Own: